The Secret Garden

8 SELECTIONS FROM THE MUSICAL
Arranged by Dan Coates

T0045160

The Secret Garden musical is based on Frances Hodgson Burnett's beloved children's novel, published in 1909. The Broadway musical premiered at the St. James Theater on April 25, 1991. After 709 performances, the run ended on January 3, 1993.

The story begins in 1906 when 10-year-old Mary Lennox becomes orphaned and is sent to England to live with her Uncle Archibald who has been heartsick since his wife Lily's death 10 years earlier. Mary has difficulty settling into his old house, especially since she hears mysterious crying at night. One day, she learns of Lily's hidden garden, which Archibald has kept locked since Lily's death. Mary asks Archibald for "A Bit of Earth" to plant her own garden, but he refuses—she reminds him too much of his beloved Lily ("Lily's Eyes"). Soon after, however, a bird leads Mary to the key to the garden, but not to the garden door. On a stormy night after hearing the crying again, Mary discovers its source—her younger cousin Colin, crippled and confined to bed since Lily died giving birth to him. When discovered in Colin's room, Mary is warned never to see him again. At the peak of the storm, she runs outside and finds the secret garden!

In Act II, Mary daydreams about "The Girl I Mean to Be" with "a place where I can go when I am lost," although she wonders if the garden is truly that place since it is so neglected and overgrown. With some help from friends, the garden is brought back to life and Colin is taken there in a wheelchair as his mother's ghost sings "Come to My Garden." Colin soon heals from the fresh air and exercise. Upon Mary's urging, Archibald returns home from abroad and finds Colin in the garden completely healthy. Colin even outruns Mary in a race! A changed man, Archibald finally accepts Mary as his own.

The Secret Garden received seven Tony Award nominations in 1991, winning for Best Book of a Musical and Best Featured Actress in a Musical (Daisy Eagan). Later productions ran in Australia (1995) and the West End (2001). Lyricist Marsha Norman and composer Lucy Simon have magically transformed Burnett's heartwarming story into one of **Broadway's Best**!

Contents

Cover Illustration by Doug Johnson © 1991

EXCLUSIVELY DISTRIBUTED BY

Copyright © MMVIII by Alfred Publishing Co., Inc.
All rights reserved. Printed in USA.
ISBN-10: 0-7390-4731-0
ISBN-13: 978-0-7390-4731-6

If I Had a Fine White Horse

Lyrics by Marsha Norman
Music by Lucy Simon
Arranged by Dan Coates

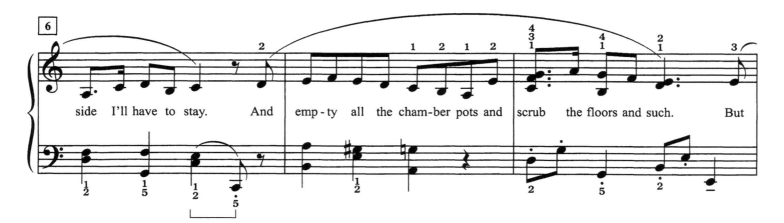

what's there to do on a fine white horse? It seems to me not much.

If I had a wood - en boat I'd
had a cham - ber - maid I'd

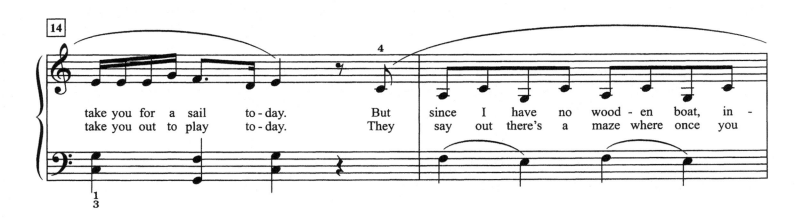

take you for a sail to - day. But since I have no wood - en boat, in -
take you out to play to - day. They say out there's a maze where once you

side I'll have to stay. And catch and kill the mice and pluck the
en - ter, there you stay. For cer - tain we'd get lost and they'd come

chick - ens for the cook. For
look - in' for our bones. And

what's there to do on a wood - en boat but
find us some time late next week. And

sit up straight and look? And
bring us tea and scones. But

wor - ry our boat would start to drift and
what if there's a clan of trolls a -

mf

float us out to sea, and
camp - in' 'neath a tree? Or

land us on an isle of gold. Oh
what if there's a pi - rate's cave? Oh

dear, oh dear - ie me. If I

rit.

a tempo

mp

1.

2.

dear, oh dear...

rit.

Oh dear - ie me. If I

a tempo

was - n't so a - fraid I'd

mf

take you out the door to-day. But talk-ing birds and tales of fair-ies keep me scared a-way. And

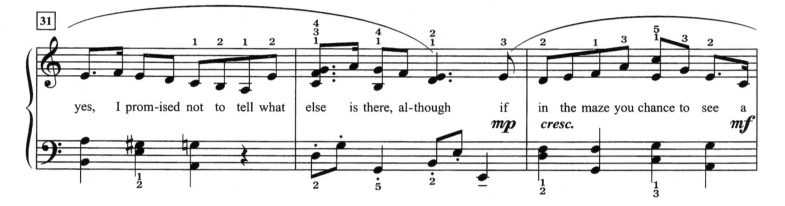

yes, I prom-ised not to tell what else is there, al-though if in the maze you chance to see a

gar-den guard-ed by a tree and meet a bird who speaks to thee, then come and tell my

fine white horse and me.

A Bit of Earth

Lyrics by Marsha Norman
Music by Lucy Simon
Arranged by Dan Coates

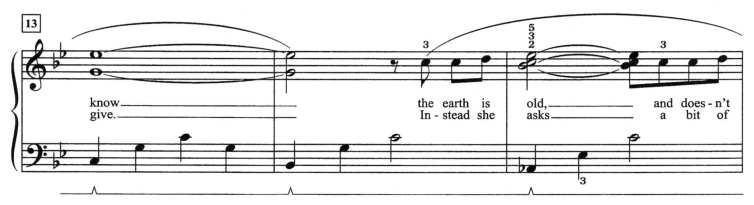

know._____
give._____ the earth is In - stead she old,_____ asks_____ and does - n't a bit of

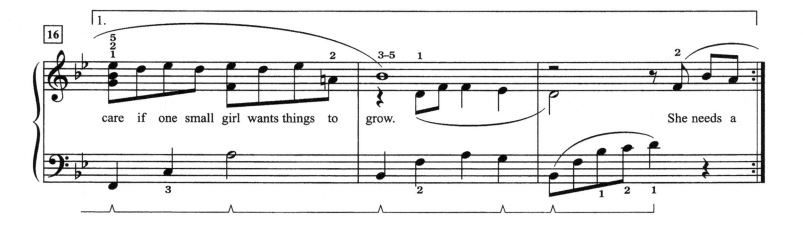

1.
care if one small girl wants things to grow. She needs a

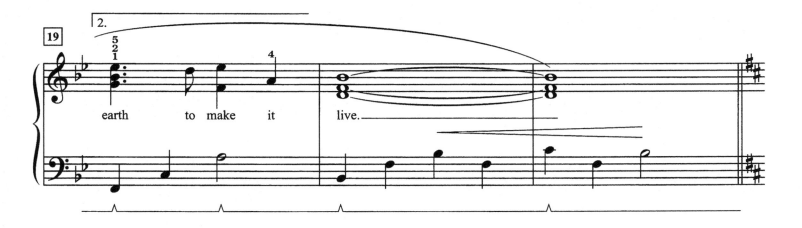

2.
earth to make it live._____

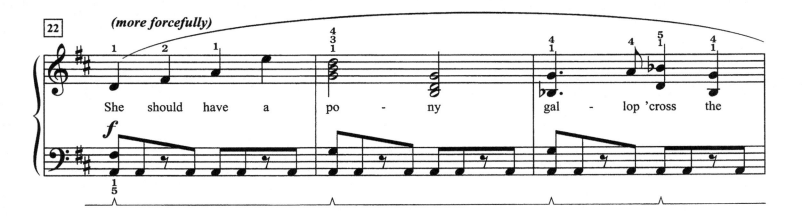

(more forcefully)
She should have a po - ny gal - lop 'cross the

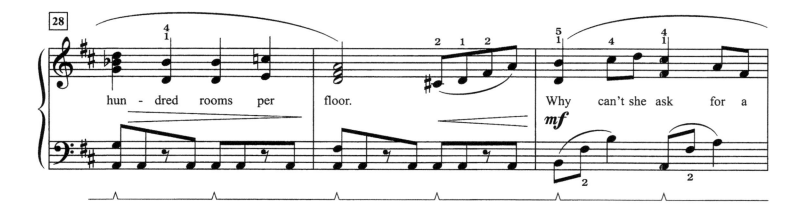

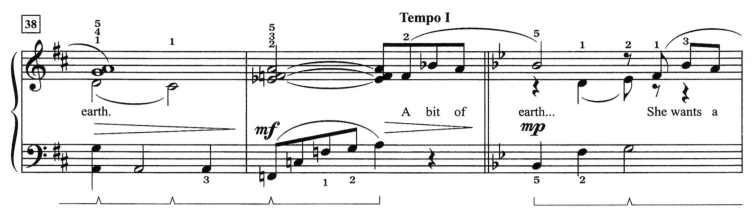

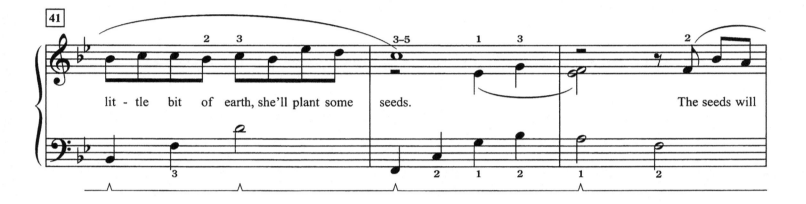

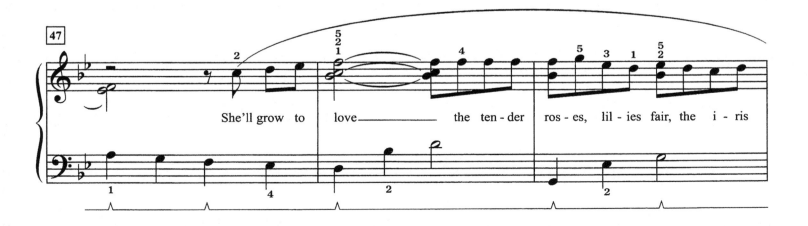

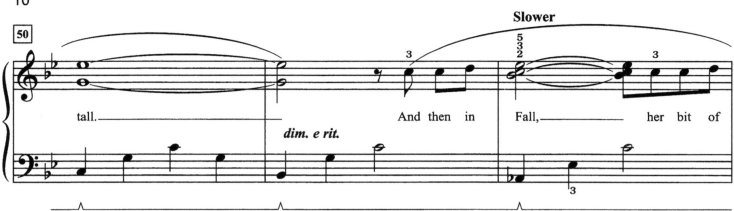

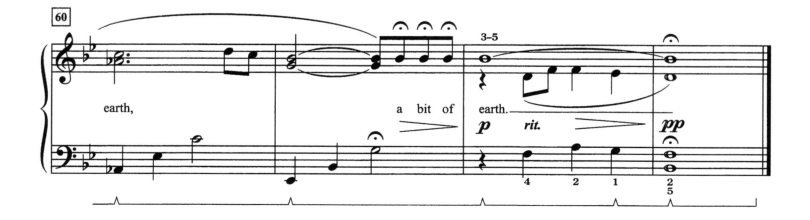

The Girl I Mean to Be

Lyrics by Marsha Norman
Music by Lucy Simon
Arranged by Dan Coates

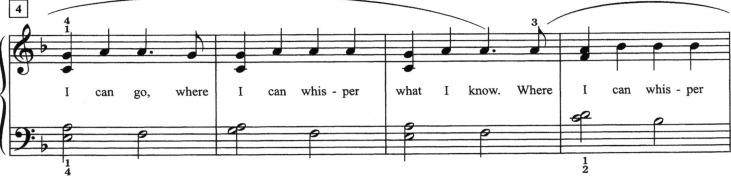

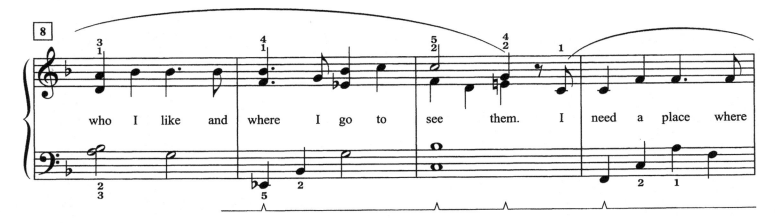

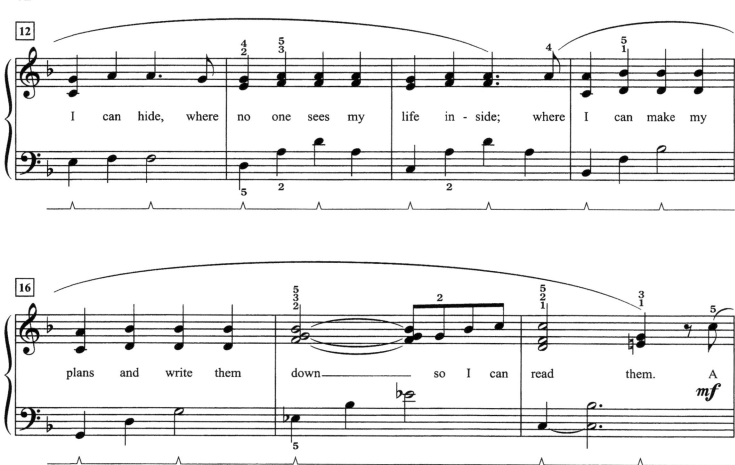

I can hide, where no one sees my life in - side; where I can make my

plans and write them down_____ so I can read them. A

place where I can bid my heart be still and it will mind___ me. A

place where I can go when I am lost and there I'll

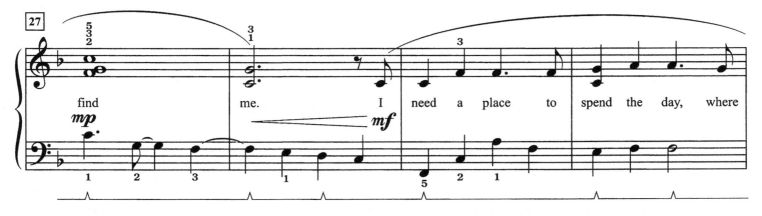

find me. I need a place to spend the day, where

no one says to go or stay. Where I can take my

pen and draw the girl I mean to

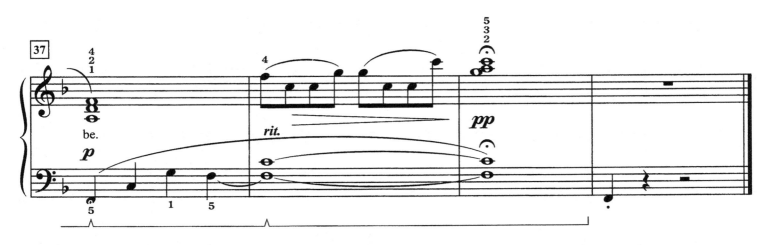

be.

Lily's Eyes

Lyrics by Marsha Norman
Music by Lucy Simon
Arranged by Dan Coates

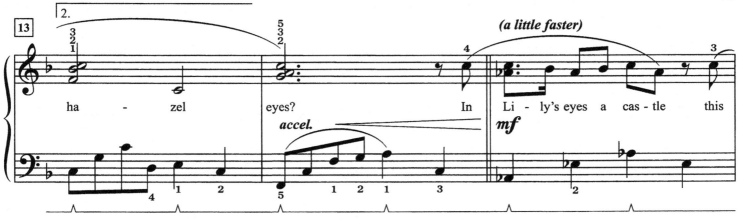

ha - zel eyes? In Li - ly's eyes a cas - tle this

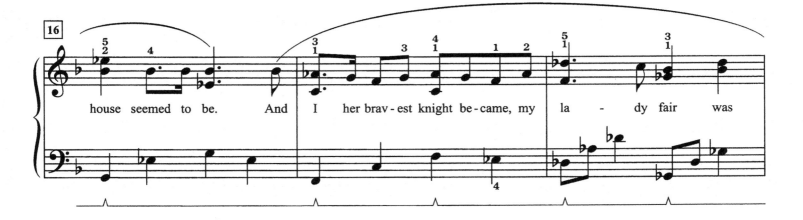

house seemed to be. And I her brav - est knight be - came, my la - dy fair was

Tempo I *(angrily)*
Dr. Craven:

she. She has her eyes, she has my

Li - ly's ha - zel eyes. Those eyes that loved my broth - er, nev - er me. Those

eyes that nev - er saw me, nev - er knew   I longed   to   hold her close, to live at last in

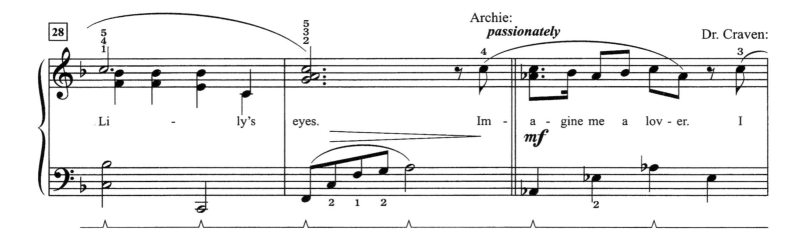

Li - ly's   eyes.   Im - a - gine me a lov - er.   I

Archie:
passionately

Dr. Craven:

mf

longed   for the day she'd   turn and see me stand-ing there. Would   God   had let   her

Both:

stay.   She has her   eyes.   She has

rit.

Dr. Craven:

Majestically

ff

Li - ly's ha - zel eyes. Those eyes that saw me hap - py long a - go._____ How

can I now for - get that once I dared to be in love, a-live and whole in

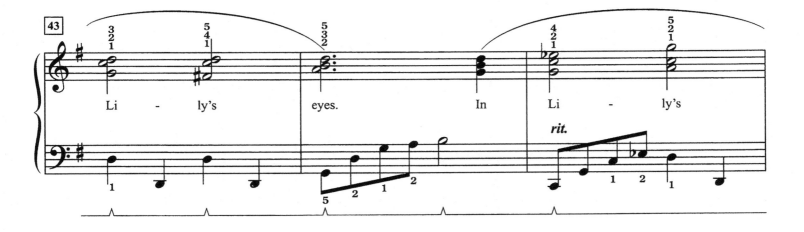

Li - ly's eyes. In Li - ly's

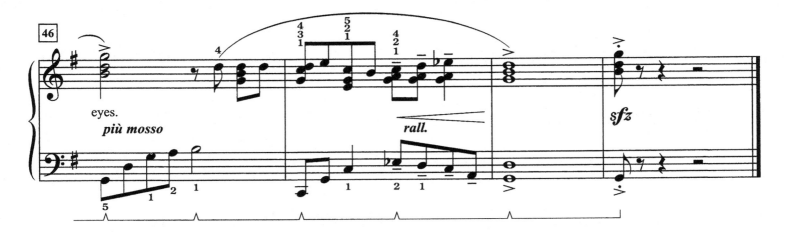

eyes.

Race You to the Top of the Morning

Lyrics by Marsha Norman
Music by Lucy Simon
Arranged by Dan Coates

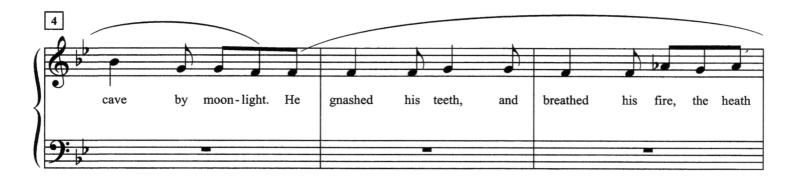

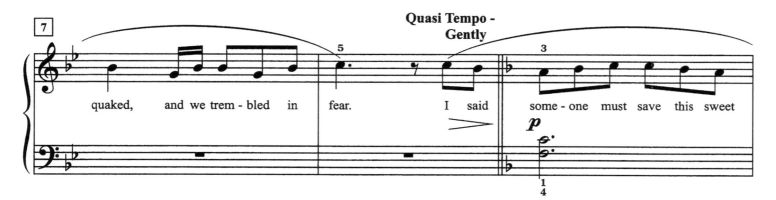

sides tied in knots, and I won! And the rest went to sleep. So, I

picked up my staff and I fol - lowed the trail of his smoke to the mouth of the

cave. And I bid him come out. Yea, for - sooth, I did shout, "Ye fool

a tempo

drag - on, be gone! or be - have." And then

meno mosso *mp*

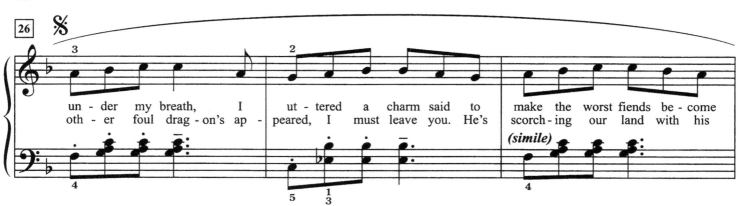

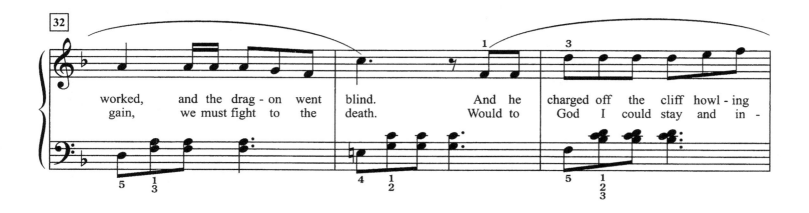

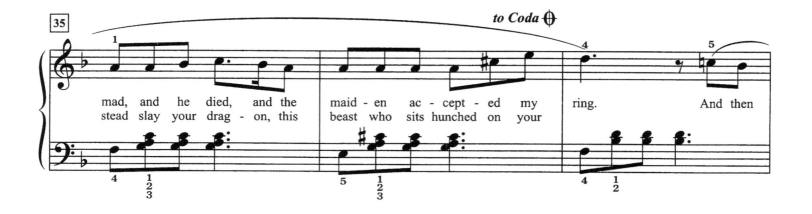

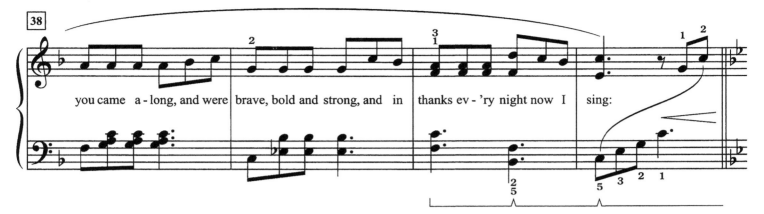

you came a-long, and were brave, bold and strong, and in thanks ev-'ry night now I sing:

mf legato

Race you to the top of the morn-ing, come sit on my shoul-ders and ride.

ped. sim.

Run and hide; I'll come and find— you.— Climb hills to re-mind— you— I

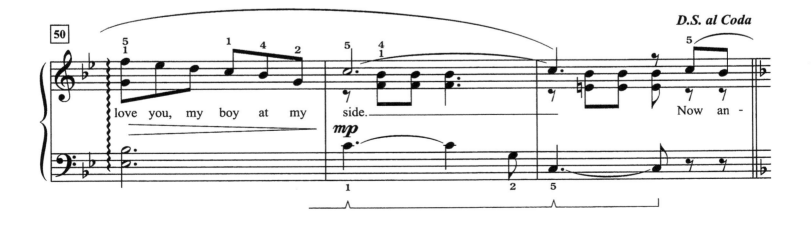

D.S. al Coda

love you, my boy at my side.

mp

Now an-

back. Would God I could wrench him a - way from your bed, or

cresc. poco a poco

mf

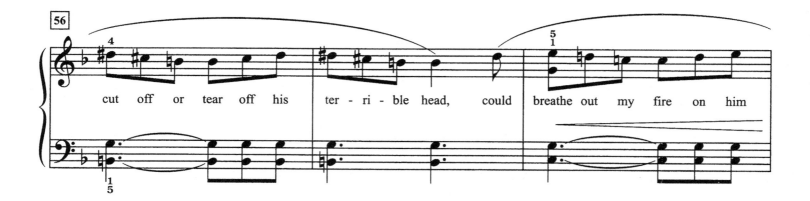

cut off or tear off his ter - ri - ble head, could breathe out my fire on him

'til he was dead, or beg him to spare you, and take me in - stead!

f

ff rit.

a tempo

mf

mp molto rit.

As it

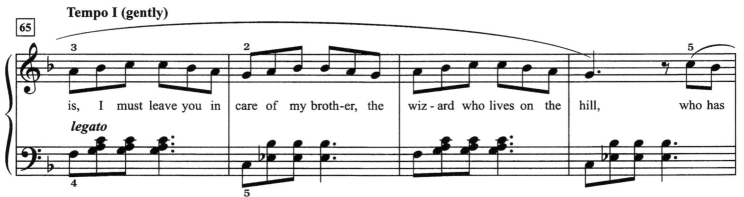

Tempo I (gently)

65 is, I must leave you in care of my broth-er, the wiz-ard who lives on the hill, who has

legato

69 prom-ised his art will soon pierce through the heart of this drag-on that's keep-ing you

72 ill. And I know that your moth-er, God bless her, would want you to

75 do as he says and grow strong. And you know that as soon as I can I'll re-turn, so be

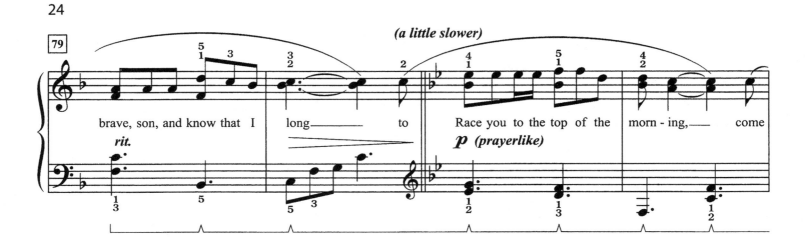

brave, son, and know that I long_____ to

(a little slower)

Race you to the top of the morn-ing,_____ come

sit on my shoul-ders and ride. Run and hide, I'll come and find__ you.__

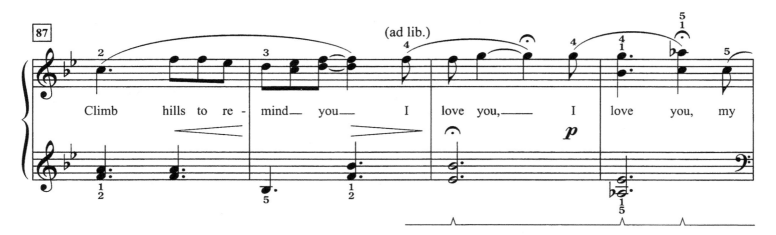

Climb hills to re-mind__ you__ I love you,_____ I love you, my

(ad lib.)

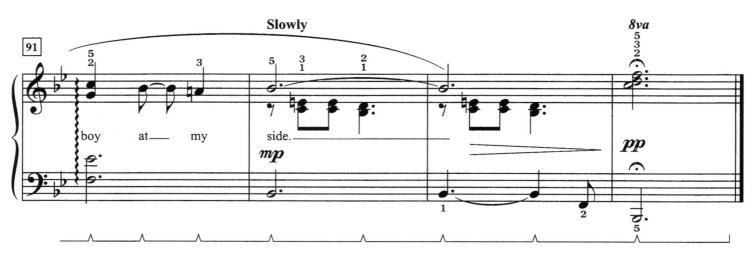

Slowly

boy at__ my side._____

How Could I Ever Know?

Lyrics by Marsha Norman
Music by Lucy Simon
Arranged by Dan Coates

Come to My Garden

Lyrics by Marsha Norman
Music by Lucy Simon
Arranged by Dan Coates

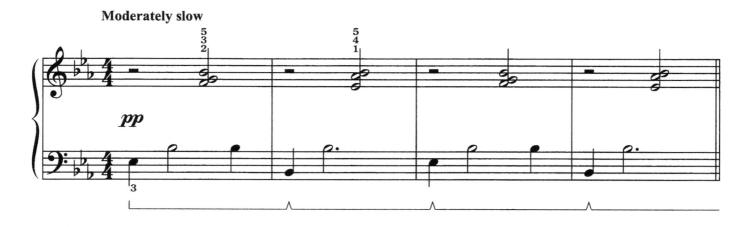

Come to my gar - den nes - tled in the hill.

There I'll keep you safe be - side me.

Come to my gar - den rest there in my arms.

mp

There I'll see you safe - ly grown and on your

way. Stay there in my gar - den where

mf

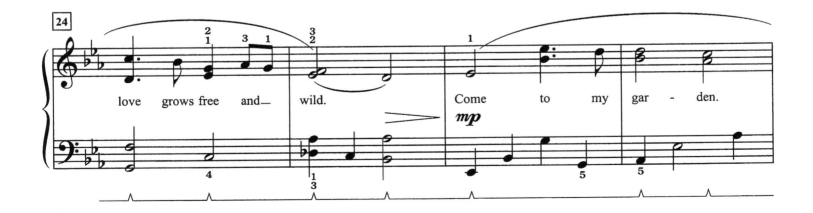

love grows free and— wild. Come to my gar - den.

mp

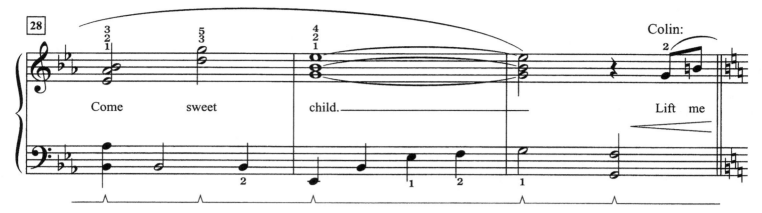

Come sweet child. Colin: Lift me

(a little faster)

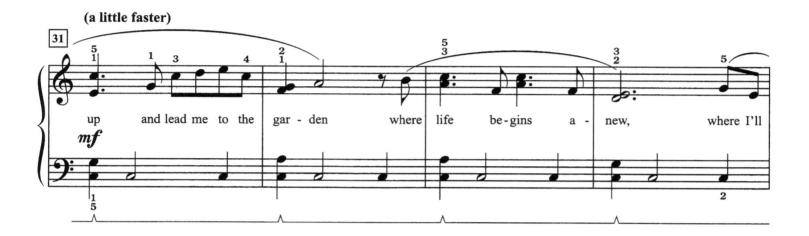

up and lead me to the gar-den where life be-gins a-new, where I'll

find you, and I'll find you love me too. Lift me

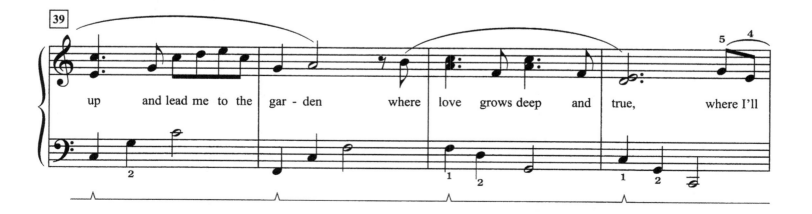

up and lead me to the gar-den where love grows deep and true, where I'll

tell you, where I'll show you my new life I will live for

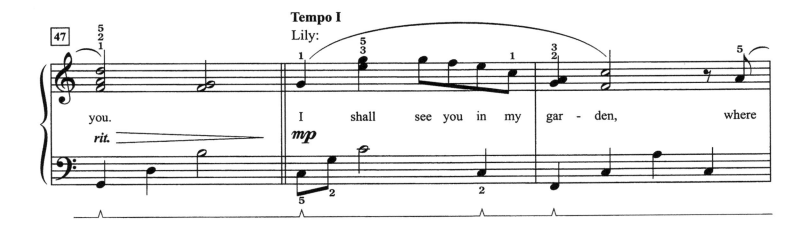

Tempo I
Lily:

you. I shall see you in my gar - den, where

rit. *mp*

love grows free and— wild. Come to my gar - den.

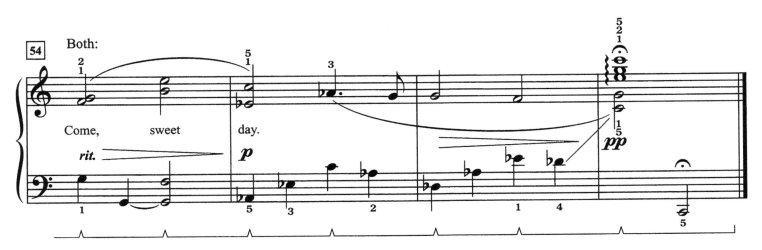

Both:

Come, sweet day.

rit. *p* *pp*

Hold On

Lyrics by Marsha Norman
Music by Lucy Simon
Arranged by Dan Coates

ter - ror in your eyes. What you do then is re - mem-ber this old thing you heard me
fro - zen to the floor. What you do then is you force your-self to wake up, and you

say: It's the storm, not you, that's bound to blow a - way.
say: It's this dream, not me, that's bound to go a - way.

Hold on, hold on to some-one stand-ing by. Hold on, don't ev - en
Hold on, hold on, the night will soon be by. Hold on,

ask how long or why. Child, hold on to what you know is true,
some - thing else to try. Child, hold on, there's an - gels on their way.

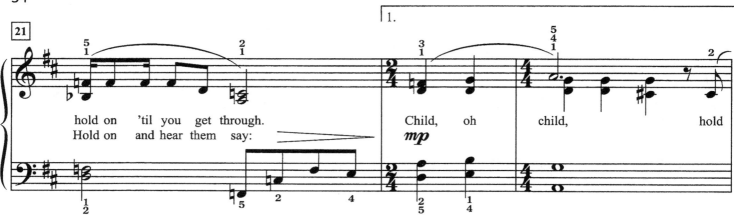

hold on   'til you get through.
Hold on   and hear them say:

Child,   oh   child,   hold

mp

on.

When you

Child, oh child.   And it

does-n't ev-en mat-ter   if the   dan-ger and the doom   come from   up a-bove, or down be-low, or

mp   *cresc.*

Heavier

just come fly-in' at you from a - cross   the   room. When you   see a man who's rag-in',   and he's

rall.   *mf*

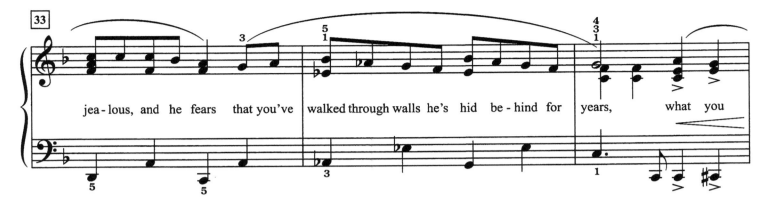

jea-lous, and he fears that you've walked through walls he's hid be-hind for years, what you

do then is you tell your-self to wait it out. You say: It's this day, not me, that's

bound to go a - way. Child, hold on, it's this day, not you, that's

bound to go a - way.